Made in the USA
Columbia, SC
29 May 2024

36300144R00057